DONATELLO'S VERSION

poems

James Scully

Curbstone Press

First Edition: 2007
Copyright © 2007 by James Scully
ALL RIGHTS RESERVED

Library of Congress Cataloging-in-Publication Data

Scully, James.
  Donatello's version : poems / James Scully. — 1st ed.
    p. cm.
  ISBN-13: 978-1-931896-31-3 (pbk. : alk. paper)
  ISBN-10: 1-931896-31-3 (pbk. : alk. paper)
  I. Title.

  PS3569.C8D66 2007
  811'.54—dc22
                                                2006028809

Printed in the U.S. on acid-free paper by BookMobile
Cover design: Stone Graphics
Donatello's *David* is in the Museo Nazionale del Bargello in
Florence, Italy

This book was published with the support of the
Connecticut Commission on Culture and
Tourism, the National Endowment for the Arts,
and donations from many individuals.

CURBSTONE PRESS   321 Jackson St.   Willimantic, CT 06226
      phone: 860-423-5110   e-mail: info@curbstone.org
                      www.curbstone.org

Acknowledgements

"Donatello's Version," "Liberation of Paris" and "The Hamlet Mess" appeared in *North Dakota Quarterly*. Earlier versions of some poems in the first section were in WORDS WITHOUT MUSIC, a limited edition, privately printed chapbook (April 2004). "Listening to Coltrane" was a limited edition broadside (Azul Editions, 2005). "Boxcars" surfaced briefly as a self-published, limited edition chapbook in May, 2006. "Dadalab," "Donatello's Version," "Qana" and excerpts from "Boxcars" are included in WE BEGIN HERE: POEMS FOR PALESTINE AND LEBANON, edited by Kamal Boullata and Kathy Engel (Northampton, MA, Olive Branch Press/Interlink Publishing, 2007).

George Amabile's suggestions have been especially helpful. Meanwhile Arlene's ongoing critiques have helped keep these writings (to borrow a phrase from Bayard Rustin) "not more straight but less crooked."

Judy Doyle at Curbstone Press has been especially patient in dealing with the many adjustments I've made to this text.

for Bob Bagg, ever *listo*:
"Formalism isn't a movement, it's a Maginot!"

contents

DONATELLO'S VERSION

1

The language which would reach them seems not to exist. But we go on writing in the forms we are used to. In other words, we still cannot believe what we see. We cannot express what we already believe.

—Christa Wolf, "Conditions of a Narrative: Cassandra"

Everything is so transparent, everything is so clear and obvious, it can make one crazy. (Leukon)

—Christa Wolf, MEDEA

LISTENING TO COLTRANE

listening to Coltrane, hearing
the original people

who abide us, sometimes
kill us

as always
we are killing them—

he blows through all
the abiding and killing

blows the send-off
we got on leaving the cosmos
the beauty of its harmony
behind us, blows

there is never any end,
there are always new sounds
to imagine,
new feelings to get at

squawking
brass, reeds, battered skin
steel wires *there is*

always the need to keep
purifying
these feelings and sounds

honking out over
       our cosmic exile

the bent strains of the original people
their long shadows riding shotgun on his wing

to give the best of what we are

ARC

"The arc of the universe is long, but it bends toward justice."
—Martin Luther King

Like a dowsing rod reaching for water
the arc of the universe
bends toward justice—

but what if there is none?

nothing in the scheme of things
as far as we
in our lifetime see
bends, surely, toward justice

what may we do then
to bend
the arc of justice
back down to earth?

it won't be with speeches,
no one needs to strain, daydreaming
after words the wind blows through

attend instead
to the coming and going
of those who are better off
with justice, than without—

all the colors, shapes, customs
being done-to unto death

but don't dwell on that,
don't cling to debris

let the slop and flow
of whatever feels like feeling
carry you along
as on a great wave cresting
an unfathomed sea of nameless peoples

who are bound to arrive somewhere

when you yourself arrive
cast up on the shore
imagine you've happened on
a folktale, or a fairytale,
the way peasants once did
in stories of yore

imagine you're a prince
or long lost princess
cast as a peasant, a noble
foundling from the sea,
the sea of peasants
storming the wicked lord's castle
saving everyone saving
the beauty of the bending universe
from the wrack and ruin
of the lord's stupidity,
his arrogance, his greed,
the dazzling panoply of his dementia
cutting words off
from the truth of the matter

imagine for that matter
Washington DC now
right now
is such a regime, its
lords ravage the countryside

imagine living this
imagine

seeing what other peasants see
feeling what they feel
having nothing left to prove
nothing more to discover
nowhere else to go

when you torch the manor house
ransack the cold cellar
tear down the whole rotten structure
imagine that

EPIGRAM

go ahead say what you want:

a shotgun blast into the dark
hitting everything and nothing

by dawn's early light

you will be digging pellets
out of the walls

SNOWBLIND

We live. Our land lies somewhere under us.

Its vastness rolls over slowly as
an SUV crashing into a snowbank.

The Constitution comes up blank,
white as a sheet. They haven't scrapped it yet.

Why bother? The thin-lipped little prince fidgets
pouts, sneers at his plastic toys, computer games—

they've taken over the house, jostling
distracting, telling him he's happy.

He is not happy. Around him words
mumble, mince, withdraw into themselves.

Desperate to please, to appease him
they disappear. *Equality, justice,* poof!

At times you stumble on one, or traces of—
like *democracy*, a real find at the flea market.

And your chest swells, you want to tell everyone,
singing or shouting, but the trauma is too much.

You reach for poetry, but it comes out verse—
you're a versifier caught in a roadblock

forced to take a sobriety test, to place
one foot in front of the other

going through the motions of taking steps
one after the other

snowblinded, on the road to disaster

LIBERATION OF PARIS

o liberation of Paris

citizens on the street
happy to see us o
beside themselves
leaping on tanks

o joyous grainy boulevards
black-&-white newsreels
o August of '44 . . .

crowing this morning
commander-in-chief
touches down
mission accomplished

o history
o endless loop

o flight suit astride the deck,
o digital perfect photo op
off sunny San Diego

o words
brazing hope,
calling victory victory

the liberation of Baghdad

o cock a doodle do
cock a doodle do

o blood in the eye
blood on the bloody beak

come home to roost

UNTITLED

"If we let our vision of the world go forth and we
embrace it entirely, and we don't try to piece together
clever diplomacy but just wage a total war . . . our
children will sing great songs about us years from now."
—Richard Perle

If we let our vision of the world
go forth

if we embrace our vision
entirely
our vision of the world

if we don't try to piece
together clever

no clever diplomacy
just war

if we just wage
total war

our children will sing
great songs of us

as of a radiance
resurrected
in the firmament

over a dead planet

NEO MANIFESTO

after Huelsenbeck

we are against spineless liberals
against reds

we are against
anti-semitic pacifists
and their islamofascist kids

against
despicable humanists
against
paleo conservative crud

we declare no end
to war without end
on the immortal stalin
and on the ever photogenic
heil hitler

we will pull down the temple
if we have to

something has to happen
something has to shake something up
for something to happen

for us to shine forth

the situation so far
is not nearly gruesome enough

DU BLUES

DU
death row

wind blow

continents countries cities
flags
wind don't know
which way wind blow

whip up sandstorm
go wherever,
4 plus billion years
it got
to go forever

number the years
of forever

eat sleep fuck
uranium forever

X ray ever hour
the hours of a life
gone catch up forever

o swindled innocence of breath

o life condemned to kill
the life it come to save
save to rob it blind
gone wait alone together

DU DU DU
death row

wind blow

TOMB OF THE UNKNOWNS

Here's the proposition:
there will be no bodies
bodies will be cremated
where, and as, they fall

these whitest of ashes
lighter than air will rise
like dust devils
whirling across the desert

bodies burned poisons burned
radioactivity burned
to eternal dust

there will be no autopsies
no evidence

no body bags delivered
to the tedium of hot tarmac,
no identical luggage descending
long conveyor belts
from the yawning void

no photos of no bodies
no waiting weeping families
wearing their Sunday best

there *will* be war, but then
there will have been no war
with no bodies

that's the deal
the proposition

The Tomb of the Unknowns
will be nowhere in particular
and everywhere in particular
like the cosmos

the cosmos too is composed
of whitest whirling ashes
riddled with slivers of bone

it can't go on forever—

this cosmos steeped in debris
deciphered
by whoops and scribbles
of spectacular graffiti
reeks of piss, ruination, ashen silences

what's left of human
is like a Quaker meeting
in an abandoned army bunker
where everyone stares at the floor:

total war

against life
against death against
past future
remembering forgetting
yesterday today tomorrow

war of all against all
to wrap up creation

come the Resurrection
the great day

bodies will be flabbergast
all all the same!
no men women children
just baby-faced *putti* cavorting
tumbling over and over
the scorcht earth
that will pass for paradise

take it or leave it it doesn't matter
the plan is in the works

DONATELLO'S VERSION

1

is unexpected:

the boy David
shamelessly naked,
one adorable leg
cocked at the knee

nonchalant
vulnerable
soft-bodied
a true killer

he wears his helmet
like a bonnet,
its pointy peak
garlanded with laurel leaves

2

the kid's a winner

little penis
big sword

standing astride
the craggy winged
head of the giant, Goliath

3

Goliath's head is peaceful,
his death like any death
is restful, untroubled
by desire or regret

4

David's skin glistens, obscurely
under a patina of melancholy

what's wrong with him

he should be dancing up and down
with joy

5

poor David
the good guy

victory is the worst thing
that could befall him

6

in the glass of his great victory,
through the loathsome mist
of world weariness

he sees himself
becoming *King* David

7

sees strings of victory
twining into distance
with strings of defeat

how he will conquer
and flee
how puff himself up
to hide

how he will dance around the sociopathic Saul

how marry, sire, beget
betrayals, adulteries,
murders, torture
prisoners raked
through the brick kiln

a weakness for poetry
will have him writing psalms
again and again

for all he has won
by this great victory
is his own disaster:

his family, his kingdom, his people
tearing apart and apart

8

he will go through life
eating flesh by the fistful

choking on shadows

9

in the improbable blood
of his great victory

he sees all this
and is famished

THE DONKEYS

for Mondo

The donkeys scream but they don't run

to the war reporter on the scene
it makes no sense

foolish beasts, donkeys

beasts of burden
with no burden
but being here
aswarm
with war machines
in the waste of Iraq

soulless
beasts
lacking the faculty
of reason

too stupid to run,
too shaggy to think
there's somewhere to run to

I too must be stupid,
still here with no reason,
another dumb animal
stuck with the sense
that all is not lost
even as all is lost

the stubborn feeling
as all goes bad

the stubborn feeling

we're still here
on our tiny feet,
our droopy eyes
black crescents
veiling and unveiling
all the soul there is—
although, in fact, there is no soul

there *is* hope for us
although there's no hope

the situation is hopeless

as the reporter leaves that place
the donkeys are still screaming

WOMAN IN BLACK CHADOR, RUNNING

the head held so high
it tilts back
a balancing act, running

eyes watery watering

like the girl in Vietnam
last century, only yesterday
still with us in a famous photo
out of her element still
throwing her head back
the same way
running naked, trailing napalm vapors
too wispy to be visible

this one is not naked though,
this is no girl
the other was slender
this is round, soft, fiftyish
this has a homely oval face
wrapped head to toe
in black fabric

this is 2003,
this is this century

running from nothing anyone can see
from no napalm
by Macy's on O'Farrell Street

like a fish out of water
limbs fanning
beating its sides, gasping

the eyes of the fish
wide with feeling,
preposterous feeling

as though a bomb has dropped
on O'Farrell Street

BABBLE

it starts with Hazel, my mother

a factory worker
looking to dress up
go out, have fun

hollering screaming

threw things
cleaned house like a demon
threw everyone out

you'll be sorry when I'm gone
you'll see!

nothing explained
nothing to ponder
no moral

*

nothing, ever,
approaching a conversation

*

it starts with Hazel then
who could be anyone
crouched at the edge of the bed
like a feral animal

3 pocketbooks on one arm,
crumbs scattered

hair crimped in a tight perm
dyed *Frivolous Fawn*
by Revlon
or Clairol

who is this person?

if looks could kill
I'd be dead

    *

the place reeks of bodily fluids
at war
with antiseptic solutions

    *

I don't know how I got to this party
I'm not working overtime

factory or party, whatever
she wants out
a ride home
shoving the walker
like a balky child

no one want money?
what's the matter with them?

waving a $5 bill,
the tiny flag she counts on
to get her out of here

if she makes it to the far door
an alarm goes off

*

baa baa baa baa baa
behind the screen

Irene, a fetal curl
dying of nothing but *old,*
babbling gargling *old old argh*
like a rockslide

old means
something falls away from you
and keeps falling

history is shit

*

how did we ever
leap into speech?

or did it break out like a ruckus
spilling into the street

regardless it goes on saying
old exhausted beating at air
still creeping up on us

Socrates having drunk hemlock
given unto death
beyond death
questions still
his voice *tweaks*
bat-like, sounding us out

Pan, another troublemaker
totally out of control
without a word still wreaks
waves of havoc

cosmic inertia
drags birth screams
through dying gasps

hauls death rattles
through agonies of rumor
where nothing is forgotten
because nothing can be forgotten

the logorrhea of eternal life
goes on and on at a party
that is no longer a party

*

Irene
slips into the unquiet stupor
we call sleep

Socrates doesn't concern her,
nor Greek

it's anyone's guess
what she has to do with Pan,
she could be his ancestor

*

for Hazel, English itself
is Greek

in the language she speaks
nothing has its own name, just
that thing! that thing there!
arthritic jabber, jabbing
a crooked finger

still she knows a thing or two
Socrates doesn't

*she knows she doesn't know
how she got to this party,
she knows no one in this place
will give her a ride home*

hence the family photos
banished from the windowsill
the paper bag mashed to the floor
the half box of crackers
the spectacles cast down

damned
for abandoning her

*

*Hazel you can't go home
the house has been sold*

*

and so, and so, what is life
is also
the abandonment of life

what's left of Hazel's
heart muscle
flutters to relax
in the slipstream of morphine

they call this 'comfort care'
this quiet dying

on this barely 4' 10" female
the factory crumpled hands
are monumental

her thick gray hair
undyed, unmangled
flows away from her face
radiating out over the pillow

her ashes falling away
from their fury

*

Irene snores, still,
through death, life, the hereafter

wadded up in the darkness of life

*

what are words for

can anyone really tell
one thing from the other
without pointing?

or is it *blah blah blah*
all Pan all the time

a 24 hour talk show
saying nothing real loud
and mean

*

you just know Socrates

the first and maybe last
extractor of human truths
from truisms
more septic than lies

is throwing up his hands

*

still if we could get past
English, past Greek

if we could crash
eternally collapsed time,
the one party we weren't invited to,
the party of matted loins
shrieking feeling
for god knows what lips
blind smashing all to bits
dizzied, with no regard
for anything or anyone

we too might find ourselves
losing ourselves

with Socrates
his moral logic
the deft limbs of it

lost in the entourage
of the bestial god Pan crushing
sentiment, scattering
qualms, family, civilizations
crackers, money, photographs
in one ecstatic panicked millisecond of babble

there, in the babble of awful truth

we might leave be
the Irene thing
the toothless mouth hole
dying endlessly of *old*
gargling ancient gravel beds

might leave the Hazel thing
that was somebody's mother
with 3 pocketbooks on one arm
and no ride home from the party
the factory, the final hospital
she never did know how she got to

. . . leave ourselves, too,
strangers and alone together
who in the end could not tell
one from the other

the voices were so mixed up

*

having shrugged off, then
language that pushes us along
like naughty children

we might meet ourselves
beyond the babble
of what was called humanity

engaging, for sake of argument,
in Pan Socratic dialogue
making no sense at all,
making all the sense in the world,

bright children growing
old with Pan

feeling in our own bones
the aching bones
of this very minor god

wrapped in his rank skin
suffused with the smell of it,
wandering corridors
leaning on our walker
agitated, asking questions
too simple for answers
too hard

how did we come to this

waving the worthless flag
the worthless money
of words that lost their meaning,
looking for a ride home

HORST BIENEK

I don't know Horst Bienek
Horst Bienek surely doesn't know me

is he still alive? someone will know

Herr Bienek was, or is, a journalist and poet,
a diminished Whitman of sorts
(though in the wide open spaces
ambling through *Leaves of Grass*
no one is diminished)

I found his defiant lines
Bienek's defiant, wishful lines
translated, awkwardly,
into a musty Penguin paperback:
we speak loudly, no one understands us,
but we're not surprised
we are speaking the language
that will be spoken tomorrow

young Bienek studying with Brecht
at the Berliner Ensemble in East Berlin

sentenced to hard labor
25 years commuted to 4
in the Vorkuta mines
of the old Soviet Union

for speaking too loudly
the awkwardly translated language
that will be spoken tomorrow

indeed some already speak it
not loudly, but in an ordinary voice
as though there's nothing to it

a language like a bowl of soup
on a cold rainy day
you eat, without thinking about it
or what it took to make this
stuff that sticks to your bones

FORENSIC FRAGMENTS

body parts
without passports

soldier
blown apart

family
charred
out riding in a car

*

bodyguards of the gods
wear body armor

what good did it do

what good
have they done

*

where's Goya?

the personality
of death
obliterated
gone
unrecorded
not one corpse

no leg no groin
no fear killing fear
not the least
smear of finger
is news

the scavengers
are so quick
so efficient

*

gods of the globe
do not speak
but echo

words of less humanity
than the howling of dogs

IN WILDERED DUST

squatters in the wildered dust
where people once lived

they have crashed
their own death camp

mistaking it
for a victory party

SCLERODERMA

Water you crave water
membranes thicken
the ravening mouth

you're coming down
with something
can a face hurt?
your face hurts
and teeth,
teeth hurt
but never like this

tongue's bunched,
shoulders ratchet
pain
there's no turning back

the more stonelike
this body that is not you
the greater the agony

you would resolve this
paradox but not now

now is no time for musing

the joints
with instinctive wisdom
contract,
set for impact

skin thickens, has to,
itself is all the armor it has

liver hardens
lungs wrack,
what's left of heart
arcane machinery, pumps
incomprehensible fluid
to no end

primeval organs
are last to go,
the digestive tract
intestines
genitalia

the moistness of future
turned off
like a faucet

now you are petrified,
you have survived

it is your destiny
to be shut up alive—

the headstone
of a stone civilization
spinning through incredible silences

you can still hear them, the silences
stone histories
stone schools
stone freedoms
stone laws
stone soldiers
stone news

stone this
stone that

everywhere

the silences
of stones that die
hurtling through space

RESURRECTION

for Arlene

It's like the Resurrection, you say
waking feeling skin

you mean
Signorelli's *Resurrection*:
bodies flexing, stretching belief
against one gorgeous, overarching
metaphysical manifestation
of human anatomy

you who know
we won't really be resurrected

when we die we die

yet now when we awaken
after all these years
in our own flesh, which
no matter how old
feels so good

the way, in the fresco,
the translucent skinned
muscular dead feel

for resurrection
we imagine only
caressing one another

here   now

where art is no more
than life, realizing itself

EXCEPT FOR LAZARUS

it is a fact, we die

it is also a fact
however old we die
the correct age for resurrection
theologically, but humanly too
is 33

the prime of life

the age Jesus
died and lived again
like a corn god
historically documented,
a god in a time
like this time—

except for Lazarus
wretched in rags
no one is resurrected
into decrepitude

no one, except

in a time like this
whose gods resurrect
only Lazarus
the walking grave

Lazarus on Lazarus
faceless heaps
of urine and blanket grease
bundled in doorways

human beings
burrowing for warmth
like so many despoiled
holes in time

by such signs we see
the gods of our time
bring death to life

that is the miracle

2

...dada literature, dada bourgeoisie, and yourselves, honored poets, who are always writing with words but never writing the word itself, who are always writing around the actual point. Dada world war without end, dada revolution without beginning, dada, you friends and also-poets, esteemed sirs, manufacturers, and evangelists...

—Hugo Ball, "Dada Manifesto" 14 July 1916

RATHER BITTERLY GRIEVED

" . . . GS rather bitterly grieved about the poor literary quality of
some of the work purveyed during the evening and expressed the
feeling that as far as it was from literary quality, so close was it to
political assertion."
    —PEN Executive Board meeting 12/6/82 (dissociating PEN from a
    poetry reading against the Sabra/Shatila massacres in Lebanon)

"Why should we hear about body bags and deaths? Oh, I mean, it's
not relevant. Why should I waste my beautiful mind on that?"
    —Barbara Bush, Good Morning America, 18 March 2003

Wake up, Poets of America!
What are you thinking of?

So far from literary quality!
So close to killing!

Violating the sacrosanct
precincts of a massacre!

Why trash poetry
with body bags and deaths?

They're not fit for newsprint
they're never on TV

why admit them
into culture, never mind verse?

What is the relevance
of body bags?

Why waste your lovely words
on such things?

DADALAB

1

the beginnings of dada
were not the beginnings
of an art
but of a disgust

so Tristan Tzara in 1922

dada came to be
the shrine of a urinal
—fountain of poverty—
signed into an art museum

a pig in an army uniform
floating overhead,
the Prussian Archangel
swimming through air
kicking its little boots, grunting
"High from the Heavens I Come"

Hugo Ball nonsense syllables
dada babble
blowing up like body parts
shoulders of words hands arms legs
of words
fleeing the Great War

weird humor

scatting lines
in the sand
between art and pissy death

2

dada judo turns
newspapers, cripples, ticket stubs
into dada ads

not to disavow art, but
to shred its
illusory transcendence

to make visible the violence
of business as usual,
its chaos and hypocrisy

laughing like mad

dada was all for
vomiting itself
out of the Great War

3

Janco Dada Museum
the heart of Ein Hod
is also built upon
art thrown up by war

a not so great war

Ein Hod = Ayn Hawd
a village in 1949
the Jews drove the Arabs
out of

its haunting emptiness
evoked, then, biblical ruins—
here was a heavensent
construction site
to mystify the bounds
of art and life

to metamorphose
dada, the art of war,
into a bubbly art movement
where, in the Dadalab,
art concocts reality—

everything is possible,
objects like a refrigerator
or a table or picture
can go through walls,
a pot becomes an animation apparatus,
the imagination spreads its wings
and soars high

says the museum brochure

and in truth, in this
art that's a kind of anti-art
everything *is* possible

the Arabs who squat on a hill
a mile or so from home
live without electricity
without water, without a road,
without wings

imagine living without wings,
and yet they do

as animation apparatuses,

present absentees
like tables or pictures
that can go through walls

because the ends of dada
like its beginnings
are not the ends of an art
but of a disgust

troubling the ghosts of Ayn Hawd
whom museum walls go through

THE LESSER EVIL

Sixty years after the fact
in Lihula, Estonia
the authorities unveil
a World War II monument

an Estonian soldier
in German military uniform

honoring those who fought
with the German fascists
against the Russian communists

a monument for those who
having to choose between two evils
chose the lesser one
according to the authorities

we too, as a decent people,
choose the lesser evil
there's no escaping it

having chosen the lesser evil
time and again
what can we do but believe
there's no way out except
make the best of a bad thing

that is why, with the Estonians
who have thought long and hard on this,
we build platforms for the lesser evil

to support those who have chosen it

CODEX GITMO

"I believe there are police; but the law here must be so different
I can't imagine what the criminals must be like."
                    —Rimbaud, "Cities II," Paul Schmidt, trans.

1

justice hoods justice
cages it

2

under armed escort
a blindfolded animal

no charges no
evidence
to fabricate this

new world
wilderness

3

an entire nation
puking its constitution
had to be numbed, gutted,
the machinations of its heart
pulled out, reconstructed
still pumping blood
to police this zoo

4

as usual
among animals
it's impossible to tell
what is criminal

we know only innocence
is out of the question

STRANGE WORDS

blindfolded
bent over a table
pants pulled down
stick shoved up
the rectum

strange word, rectum
stranger by the day

unreasonable residue
of rectify and rectitude
not right, but narrow

I couldn't scream
but when I did
I couldn't stop

how will the poem
approach this

strange word, poem
stranger than rectum

a panhandler
suspiciously well-dressed:
spare a word?
a syllable or two?
speaking what
might be Greek

looking for something
real, but not too, a little
something the poem can use

yet passing through
this netherworld
of beastly silence
the scream goes on,
spares nothing

STAR CHAMBER

by tradition
justice wears a blindfold,
sword in one hand
scales in the other

sometimes, a book
in the crook of her arm
or under the armpit

but print blurs
words
swamp with ink

ink
darkens to blood
words drown in

*

sky is a dome of stars
with no constellation
for justice

when we look up
into the darkness
that's best to see in
justice is what
we feel the absence of

*

to constellate justice
we'll keep the sword
write off the law books
unhook the fulcrum
from the scales

we have no scales
to weigh
the metaphysical difference
the palpable indifference
between innocence and guilt

*

justice being blind
needs no blindfold

still we apply it
for poetic truth

*

as if justice were a person
and not the personification
of a system

tearing off archaic robes

dropping the blindfold
slipping into fatigues
pulling on rubber gloves

to strip prisoners
down to the cocks
she points at

her pathos
grinning for the camera

siccing
our dogs on

　　　*

we will think about this
a long while and then

we will stop thinking

THEY

Sadr City, 28 August 2004

took him inside the house
detained
his family on the patio

cut off the plastic cuffs
shot him in the head, twice,
dragged him out

his wife
hysterical, wailing
throwing dirt up in the air
beat on herself with both hands

they watched, shocked
she placed her baby
on the bleeding body

this had not occurred
to the video wars
racketing the screens
of their video games

yellow ribbons
neatly looped and swallow-tailed
on trees and cars, boding
their soldiers coming home
had envisioned nothing
as mad

as a baby's blind warmth
on a man's corpse

BOXCARS

1

Christmas '43
I'm six everything exists

in pristine space

the brand new
Lionel electric train on an oval track
speeds through the straightaway
    slows
at the curve
        snakes away
in a jumble of colorful boxes

... reappears
as a steam engine,
a ponderous black beast
        yoked
to rough wooden boxcars
bucolic as oxcarts

the older I will get
the earlier the times I will live in

2

the duration of the war
creaking the spur line behind our house
        real trains crawl by nightly
                whooing

through my bedroom
boxcars of munitions, rifles, sidearms
Colt, High Standard, Winchester's, Marlin Firearms . . .

V-J Day we hanged
Tojo from a cherry tree
and burned the carcass

the trains went away . . .

I slept
to the gurgled *cooing*
of pigeons under the eaves, clearing their throats

days we scavenged the abandoned tracks
like scrapyard dogs
in a dream park of bluish cinders
cratered, razory—
we kept
cutting ourselves, not noticing
we were so excited
on the iron path to the ends of the known world
crunching underfoot—
past
tar-soaked crossties, coded zinc medallions hammered in,
rail spikes in iron collars
rusting away
in scraggly weeds

us crashing through
the watery-stalked clumps of junk bamboo

3

when was it boxcar rumors
began to fill with Jews?

nondescript
    as sunflower seeds
shoveled into a mouth of blackened teeth
they disappeared into the death camps
we knew only as concentration camps

decades later, no one could think boxcars
without thinking Jews

     4

Saturday matinee us kids
    licorice sticky
watch the Pathé news

The Eyes Of The World
a camera on a tripod swivels
    its gigantic
        lens at us
the screen blacks out

GIs LIBERATE THE CAMPS

soldiers unravel limbs skin bones hair
lift the striped pyjamas, stack
carefully, awkward, not wanting to touch
or break
    the staring things inside them
onto truck beds

bewildered are
    the soldiers in helmets
beholding the bewilderment of the pyjamas

the little round caps
set squarely
on the tops of shaved heads

5

even so, under the heaps
of cheap baggy cotton
there is a prior life,
the life before this one

hiding, holding its breath

. . . in handcolored
postcards from beach houses,
the spas and mountain resorts
of another era

the dank, tingley
        savor
of bathhouse wood—
                shivers
ravaging the air
        unnerving
the loins at summer's end

black-&-white under the merciful haze
of sepia

grainy photo faces
weighed down in hopelessly old-fashioned clothing
the layers, they wear, of all they can carry
the murmurous shuffle of a stadium crowd
        crushing itself,
ordinary seeming people, despite

the uniform silence:
        faces like tremulous leaves
curled whitely, sensing change in the weather
of a place with no trees

        6

watching an SS officer's home movie
exhibit the nakedness
        sizes, ages, whitenesses
of normal healthy women
lined up for the showers

the naked always women
never men

what's shocking is
        what's shocking:
they're supposed to be starving
but aren't

they're healthy! why kill them?

the kid watching this
        is struck
half a century later older thinking

what if they'd been sick
all skin, bones & eyes?

it wasn't the murder
        got him, but
the meaninglessness of it

how he imagined
       ghastly death
could not comprehend bodies
so banal, so lined up and naked

7

I'm sixteen, witness to
this art house double-bill:
       the calm before
offscreen, the slaughter
followed by Bergman's *Naked Night*

some as yet unfathomable
       genius
dreamed the program up

which begins, as it must, with the flesh
     of women
queued peaceably, uneasily, to enter
the death scramble
of their own unutterable screams

      . . . watched by unseeing
soldiers who give nothing away

they too are being watched

neither women nor soldiers dream of
how could they
      this weird Bergman film:
the carnival madness of a raging bear
      the mangey symbol
               rattling its cage—

neither women nor soldiers conceive, how could they,
    Bergman closing in on
the pathos of a clown half-carrying half-dragging
                home, in his arms,
the naked crazy wife who has walked into the river
under a hillside of soldiers
out for gunnery practice

the soldiers
laughing, jeering

powdery sweat beading
the clown's desperately whited face . . .

the naked women
the Nazis
        guarding them
in the skincrawling abyss of their decorum
are still as period pieces
at the end of the known world

        8

how is it
the undressed bodies of long dead human beings
turn spectral, like dirty air
        catching the light

half-buried
awful treasure

        9

mornings in the mirror
        I see

a daguerreotype
staring back at me

not really my face
but an unreconstructed
        history,
the obsolescent technology
of eyes, nose, lips
light and shadow

breathing in out in
        out
the humanity
of dirty air

        10

        those others
                the naked
staring at the backs of their own heads,
not daring to face one another

they don't know what to think either

still I ask them: *what are you thinking?*

like the lens called Pathé
        Eyes Of The World
they turn on me, and say: *lots of things*

        11

what is it, '67? 1967?
I'm thirty, nothing is pristine

I look for them again
                they've fled!
taken their nakedness with them

the train so long now
no one sees the end of it

                        boxcars loom,
a chain gang of Memorial Horrors
        hitched together
on a transworld rail tour

going round the world
        as a local . . .
like a milk train
                it stops
at every town it passes through,
a bloody road show—
                chronic reproach
coming and going, the haunting
        refrain
whose final destination is a mystery

on the implacable sides of the boxcars
        HOLOCAUST
in thick black Gothic script
stares out, near yet distant

within: human remains lie scattered, withered,
boneyards dug up
                to people
museums of death, the uncomprehending dead
                        dragged from sleep
to be taken where now? *they had not dreamed of this*

12

more night more fog rolled in

the natural light of the world
obsessed
          with an agenda
turned, merely, to *lighting*

the world was coming down with something
film noirish
          always on the run, running
from something

my heart beat hard
caught redhanded
          witnessing
the immolation of human history—

HOLOCAUST
          descending
dead ending everything and everyone into something
          shameful and shameless
howling like a mind afire

13

I came to in a boxcar,
there was nowhere else to be

others there were, also transported
amid muffled
          coughing, breathing
trying not to make a scene

. . . winding through the '50s, '60s, '80s
                Y2K fantasm
switchbacked into the '70s, tunneled from light
        to dark into the breathsucking '40s '30s vortex
shabby, breaking broken glass—

HOLOCAUST fires gasped
air out of the air
                the engine
        seemed to stoke itself
with bodies of ordinary people,
the long dead, first, in shrouds of clothing,
then the sad-eyed, darkly artful, the sullen
        leaving behind
striped stick figures
in terrible baker's caps
serving now no further purpose

we others, rattled
        jerked
every whichway
we too were being consumed

human fuel for human fire

        combusting history
as in the belly of a great ancient conquering army
            an armored column
of boxcars, logistical genius, a triumph of misery
        over future
over the simple recognition
of human

surpassing all
        the peasant
holocausts along the way,
unprepossessing ethnic cleansings,
dusty provincial genocides, records lost

crimes against humanity
left for nameless

eyes, noses, lips
never again
to relate a human face

rolling past all that now

banged against brain-scarred walls
bruised, slivered, swaying
            past insignificant bloodlettings,
                    the merest whispers of them
sinking into marshes deserts jungles steppes
walled-off parts of cities
where they are heard from hardly ever

and then, never

clickety-clacking
clickety-clacking

clickety-clacking

        14

I must have dozed off, everyone must have
            next we know
we're backsliding, worn wheels jetting sparks

the Holocaust local weighing tons
becomes, like fate,
a global munitions train

train that stopped running
that evening
we hanged Tojo from the cherry tree
and burned him in kerosene

in reality we were passing Guatemalan
or were they Mayan
anyway kids, mothers, Nicaraguans, Salvadorans, Chileans

black South Africans unloading the arms
that will kill themselves

and then, I swear,
the boxcar walls were plastered with American flags,
we'd hitched a ride home in a cargo plane
the GIs in cardboard boxes like freight draped in old glory
to be offloaded, forklifted onto a loading dock—
American Holocaust flags streaming someplace still
where all the blacks were gone
converted enlisted drowned or locked up somewhere,
scraps of Indians swept off
into a dreamland without clocks or windows
confined to casinos
as in a time travel machine
creating its own warp
on its own track

coursing now
over Cambodian skulls with ID photos, through Rwandans
o god Rwandans in '59, '63, '93, '94, '95
huddled inside a church,

machetes taking their sweet time awaiting
      the decency of dark
to come in

      15

boxcars rocking past with such abandon now
mythic, mystifying
            casting their history behind them
no throwaway Gypsies, no communists, no Jews,
no Poles or homosexuals sharing
      pink triangles,
no living room except
for money and weapons

no room for the absence
of unutterable screams

      16

even to speak this
is unspeakable

to speak
of Sudanese women and children in the gorgeous wraps
of National Geographic—
            skeletal young girl, lustrous skin
stretched tight on bone frame like a black paper kite
      grounded, staring
through airless umber haze of dust and flies
                  tells as nothing else
            how fantastic how beautiful creation is

to speak of the atrocity
of the aesthetic

because beauty shows through
        even this
the way a column of smoke
gushes up
on its own exhaustion
wreathing an agony of shadows
                Hiroshima
                        human
fingers ignite like flares
dead black pieces flaking onto the road
                                leading to the river

because this too is unspeakably human

the women are war-raped
while other women
        of other colors
the same color
sing the rapists on

because how heady are
the rails singing and clicking beneath our feet

clickety clacking
Congo
Nigeria
Chechnya

boiling flesh Uzbekistan

speechless bodies
flashing by on either side

metal skinning metal
into the 21st century

its children
the moving target
its children
its children
its children

locked into
the racketing
boxcars of Holocaust

17

look, what should have been
light is darkness

the lessons of the Holocaust
        learned by rote
practiced over and over in the mirror
shatter their own image

soldiers of the Holocaust
cossack shadows rampage
                across and across
the Holyland they dreamed
driving two-legged beasts
to extinction

18

in this dream, your dream,
we exist as *present absentees*
                insects
        in perennial rubble
under a heaven of unforgiving genesis

whatever tells of us
who used to be human
is razed, obliterated, walled-up
     crushed
by bulldozers bigger than a house

    19

your dream is a nightmare
because we are in it

we crowd streets between curfews
your tank clanks through
    slowly
sprays us with DDT
as though we're another species

we could be another species

we are born in boxcars,
the bad faith of boxcars,
the *carte blanche* of boxcars,
bundled under munitions
side by side
with dug up naked bones

our fathers mothers grandparents
uncles aunts, kids old as
stones, as dirt, as names, oranges, hearts
older than histories
are heaved up into them
    as wanderers
in battered trunks called *the demographic problem*

as who on earth isn't
a demographic problem

the more we are, the less we matter

look at us
we carry no weight
        we miscarry
your missiles in the marketplace
we who have no missiles

with us, now, the ghosted boxcars of the Holocaust career
        so screamingly light
like a bad joke gone really bad
they threaten to fly, fly, dragged
                off the rails, to crash
this only life on earth we are passing through

because when our species ends
yours does too

GENBAKU SHI

"died by atom bomb"
genbaku shi
engraved on
upright cenotaph

genbaku shi genbaku shi genbaku shi
over and over
broken record
in record limbo

"died by atom bomb"
"died by atom bomb"
"died by atom bomb"

nothing else
no who no
why no subject
to deliver the sentence

no killed, killed
can't imagine
being this bad

just, died by

the heavy bone
would be that of the teacher,
beside it
lie
bones of little heads

no matter words
cram the slab
enact the punishment
as on a blackboard,
writing to eternity
for having been died

"by atom bomb"
"by atom bomb"
"by atom bomb"

like unruly kudzu
made to repeat
identical Japanese
syllables in lieu of leaves
top to bottom
right to left
which is not natural
to kudzu

genbaku shi
genbaku shi
in straight lines
gone mad

running up and
down over the rough face
of some kind of stone

WILD TREES

"The world was all before them, where to choose..."
—Milton, PARADISE LOST, XII

it was late in the day

we came on
the obvious: crab apples,
blood clots of rusted fruit

these aroused in us
nostalgia
for what never existed
and never would

beyond, we noticed other trees
orchard apples abandoned
to their own devices
and pitiless desires

hollow trunks
twisted, fruitless, leafless
sprouting twigs and twiglets
with slow, maniacal fury . . .

they explained nothing
illuminated nothing

     *

in this late light, explanation
insults intelligence

illumination blinds

*

ahead: skeletal elms

scabrous trunks
lining a dirt road long after
the paved avenues of their heyday
are worn to rubble,
the trolley rails torn up

*

one after the other
a line of crows by the water
flap flaps off—

the eschatological sheen
we can't see through
or into, because
it reflects the death of everything

is ripped away
by flying black rags

not hurrying, exactly, but hustling
to get something done somewhere
who knows where or what

barking at one another

*

unlike, now, the placid
wildness of cows congregated
at the farthest, lowest corner of a pasture
not sitting or browsing, but

pressing some urgent concern
at an emergency meeting . . .

I'd no sooner inquire of that crowd
than a skirmish line of crows
combing a meadow, tossing straws in the air

that way lies madness

*

let the trees tree
madness

let the world world
I love it that the crabs
are inedible

the slender elms on either side,
fountains of stillness,
reach out to announce an arch over the mind

through which let the crows crow

*

the bearing of those cows
suggests
a Giotto fresco of Dominican friars,
massive brown robes and wide-brimmed hats
sheer bulk and color
speaking nothing but big body language

*

I myself came late to explanation

four years in a Dominican high school
I never thought to wonder
who was Saint Dominic,
the nuns never thought to tell us

*not about Dominic
nor, later, Savonarola
stirring up the bonfire of the vanities
not to be bought off
by the pope's offer of a cardinal's hat*

"A red hat? I want a hat of blood."

*so hanged
& burned*

*

the nuns had no more to do with that
than Mary did with Joseph—

or did they know better
than try to explain it

*

because wherever they turned, they saw
we all did, under the same dispensation
the Virgin Mary on a pedestal
arms spread wide, and low,
palms up in perpetuity,
robes blue and white

above the bank of vigil candles,
flames drafting over the glass rims
licking the gloom above
the glowing red cups they were set in—

her bare foot still
crushes the serpent's head,
her expressionless complexion
still looks
time into cold, unwrinkled space

gone straight to heaven
without passing through death
as even Jesu did, I mean
that Mary, she was one *wild* tree

who in her muteness
as darkness flies up
gives away nothing, except
the endlessness of nothing,
hence the futility of longing

Mary, in whom
all questions died before they could come to mind

THE HAMLET MESS

Everyone rewrites Hamlet,
even the chimpanzees.
Well not the whole Hamlet, not chimps,
but at least the beginning.
For them, that itself is an achievement.
Hunting and pecking on an old typewriter
one day they find
they have a hairy finger in the Hamlet pie.
There's a play about this,
a thinking person's *Planet of the Chimps*.

Nearly everyone takes a stab at it.
Not to get it right
—after all, Hamlet himself didn't—
but to get it wrong in the right way,
the way that suits them.

Take the Arab Hamlet, Hamlet
without make-up, dying.
Of course his whole life is dying.
He finds out secrets that are killing him
and blows them up. Like Ur-Hamlet does.
And lives in a rotting state, or none at all,
where the physical world is so metaphysical
living is a contradiction in terms.
"Don't bring the curtain down," he pleads,
as though he had curtains, as though
he could die before he's blasted away
by the lies that make up the Hamlet play—
as though he weren't caged up
in reality, the last sky, beyond

the playhouse of the fictional Hamlet's
dinky stage with its dark, crampt wings.

Naturally the Israeli Hamlet is proscribed
by the Israelis. He exists, yes
but only on a list, a sacred scroll
which may not be revealed—
an exceedingly Hamlet-like predicament.

The Israeli Hamlet may be the purest
Hamlet on God's troubled earth.

The Polish Hamlet is another kettle of
whatever. He tells ghost stories to children
(he's the only Hamlet who has them)
stories about a rat behind the arras
while the kids wonder, what's an arras?
Him talking talking, yet
thinking thinking, not telling them
he's the Polish Hamlet, it's *he* who dwells on
the milk-smooth thighs of the queen mother—
keeping mum, too, about the poor mad girl
the English Hamlet looked to death.

As for that question about hatpins
and choosing to be or not to be
it is, he says, a crude stupid joke
"to the man of today." To get the joke
though, we'd have to be Polish.

We'd have to come back
from the dead, plodding yet again
into the world.

The German Hamlet on the other hand . . .
but which German Hamlet?

There are so many.
Often the German Hamlet isn't Hamlet
but Ophelia whose scream tunnels the water,
her spell compels a bullet
to shatter against a willow leaf.

But typically, stereotypically,
the German Hamlet is a machine
tearing its own image apart.
Now that's a Hamlet. It rips
idiot Elizabethan questions
into fustian scrap.
And drinks on it.

Which leads straight to the Russian Hamlet!
There's a vast, deep hinterland.
We will never run out of Russian Hamlets.
Like the original, they fidget. Carp.
Here's one loves the role, but not the play.
He wants the script changed!

But by far, hands down,
the most fascinating, pathetic,
feelingly ridiculous Russian Hamlet
sleeps in the same room as you
but in another bed. He doesn't sleep
of course, nor do you, but goes over
his shallow, insignificant, worthless
unoriginal life with such great energy
and passion, it startles the provincial
pomposity stranded in the next room.
Strangely, you wish he wouldn't shut up,
this bundle of nerve-ends, but he does.
In the morning, he's gone.

Doubtless there are other Hamlets.
Argentinean, Nigerian, Indonesian,
a Japanese in a video arcade playing
killer games with the state of his dreams
and, possibly, the state of the princess.
But if so, I don't know them.
Or did, and forgot.

One thing is certain: only the Americans
do not write, or rewrite, Hamlet.
If they do it's a family film
with murder and incest, nothing huge.
Yet how imagine a Hamlet who does not
agonize over picky little things all balled up
in the state of the world? What world
might an American Hamlet agonize over?
And what's to ponder, or notice, about
a billow of clothing, some weeds,
a glimpse of flesh and hair
drifting down a river?

Nor do they agonize
over the ghosts of their fathers
or worry what's rotten, or what to kill, even though
like the young Prince Hamlet, wherever they pass
something bad happens, and after that
something worse.

Hamlet himself, only just realizing as much,
is puzzled to discover his own hand
in his own blood.

O SAY CAN YOU SEE

O president of madness
    that pulled the towers down
and gave your soldiers gladness
    to torture all that's brown
    o torture all that's brown

the goddam piece of paper
    lies in blood and rust,
your politicians labor
    to suck up what they must
    o suck it up, they must

sweet dreamers wake up poorer
    black folk drown out of sight,
reporters pimping horror
    manage to do all right
    you dictate, while they write

god's lawyers give your word
    poof! people disappear!
this empire of the absurd
    will rapture us, we fear
    to cells in the stratosphere

O prince in corporate rags
    you are your mother's son
hiding the body bags
    to bury what you've done
    o bury what we've done

THERE IS NO TRUTH TO THE RUMOR

there is no truth to the rumor
the Constitution's
a goddamned piece of paper

it's not vegetable, but animal
dressed as parchment—

invented in Pergamon
in not yet Turkey
3rd century BCE
when the papyrus ran out

Ionian Greeks called sheets of it
diphtherai, or 'skins'

by the time of Herodotus
writing on skins was common

Assyrians and Babylonians
in what for now is called Iraq
were already writing on skins

writing and rewriting
past traces of earlier writing
on recycled skins
they'd scrubbed and scoured

they wrote what they believed
mattered   •
on something meant to last

rabbinic books weren't books
but scrolls of parchment, as
were, later, early Islamic texts

great civilizations as living cultures
writing themselves on skin

writing rewriting
laws, histories, religions, all
on cured skin: split
sheepskin, goatskin, cowhide,
horsehide, squirrel and rabbit

aborted calf fetuses
hairless through and through
as is the skin of angels
would be reserved
for especially precious stuff

yet regardless of grade, without exception,
skin being mostly collagen,
the water in ink or paint
would melt it slightly
creating a raised bed for the writing

like welts on a body
showing what's been done to it

even today, to write on parchment
or color it
the tiniest bit watery
is to bring all this doing up

each writing a rewriting
overwriting the life of skin

so if its breath is gone, its muscles
having lost all sense of purpose
bereft of heart and liver, still
in the heat and humidity
of human and meteorological exertion
it buckles, shifts, sweats and squirms

uplifting a little,
like from a death bed,
giving lie to the rumor
the Constitution is a piece of paper
damned or not

because, even dead, it will let us know
this was a living matter
that was being painted up, written off on
chewed by dogs and lied over

QANA

where the wedding was
where water turned to wine
where the best was saved
for last

shsh   they're trying to sleep
in the dark wood
of dreamless dreaming—
coughing farting snoring sighing
turning over

where the wedding was
the rolling storm
that is not a storm
flies over

it doesn't feel much
to drop a bomb—
a slight bump
under the wing

the thing is done—

their deaths
like little yapping dogs
rush out
into the nerve-endings of the universe

the bodies stay put,
impossibly still

so it was said in school
Macbeth doth murder sleep—
with so much life to kill
there's no room for sleep

in Qana
where the wedding was
those who sleep, die

the future of sleep
is buried alive

in Qana where the wedding was
the murdered in their sleep
wake just long enough to die
to become the woods
where the wedding was . . .

they are on the move now,
which is impossible

these impossible dead
growing out of their deaths
into an army of trees

THE ANGEL OF HISTORY

"His eyes are staring, his mouth is open, his wings are spread."
—Walter Benjamin

blown backwards
into the future

he beholds only
the past
dragging after him

what a catastrophe
the furious wind
hurls at his feet

helpless before it

his wings are spread—
fanned flat
with the sharp snap
of terrified sails

how will he fold them
feather on feather
before the torrent
of shock waves from paradise?

him
on his wretched wings
helpless to help
anyone
or anything

what he shouts
is spittle
torn from his mouth

himself, ever only
a single breath ahead
of where he has been

where even now

the surge of broken bodies
is breaking over him

filling his eyes, his mouth, his ears
with creaturely whispers

crushing with love the wings
that have caught him up
in so much misery

DADALAB
"High from the Heavens I Come": Christmas carol verse on John Heartfield and Rudolf Schlichter's Prussian Archangel. Hugo Ball, with Emmy Hennings, was seminal to Dada.

The Dadalab is in the Janco Dada Museum at Ein Hod, 20 km south of Haifa. Dadalab is advertised as "an interactive exhibition in which everybody can assume the role of a Dada artist, break the bounds of conventional art and engage in interdisciplinary creation. In the Dadalab everything is possible...."

DU
Like WWI mustard gas, depleted uranium (DU) attacks everyone, including those who deploy it—killing slowly from the inside out. Victims breathe and ingest the toxic radioactive gas and particles released by uranium weapons, which burn on impact. Unlike mustard gas, DU is truly omnicidal—destroying even the future as it is passed on through semen. There is no cure.

GENBAKU SHI
Genbaku Shi ("died by the atom bomb") is written over and over on a tombstone at Mitaki-yama in northern Hiroshima.

"The heavy bone..." Verse by Shoda Shinoe engraved on the pedestal/cenotaph for teachers and children of the elementary school who died from the atom bomb.

From HIROSHIMA-NAGASAKI: A Pictorial Record of the Atomic Destruction (1978) Hiroshima-Nagasaki Publishing Committee (Committee of Japanese Citizens to Send Gift Copies of a Photographic and Pictorial Record of the Atomic Bombing to Our Children and Fellow Human Beings of the World).

O SAY CAN YOU SEE / THERE IS NO TRUTH TO THE RUMOR
November 2005. When, on Constitutional grounds, White House aides objected to renewal of certain provisions of the Patriot Act, Bush responded: "Stop throwing the Constitution in my face! It's just a goddamned piece of paper!"

QANA
Thought by some to be the biblical Cana. Modern Qana is the site of two massacres—the first in 1996, when Israeli shelling killed 106 sleeping refugees in a UN compound. Ten years later, on 30 July 2006, the Israelis bombed a basement shelter where Lebanese citizens were sleeping. Of the 56 people killed, 34 were children. The bomb, a laser-controlled BSU 37/B "bunker buster" with a depleted uranium (DU) warhead, was supplied by the U.S.

IAF General Dan Halutz: "What do I feel when I drop a bomb? A slight bump in the airplane." Adding: "By the way, I sleep well at night."

The Israeli military claimed the Hizbullah-led Lebanese resistance camouflaged its rocket launchers with moveable trees. Coincidentally the flag of Lebanon features a cedar tree.

Also by James Scully

MODERN POETICS, ed. (1965) Reissued as MODERN
POETS ON MODERN POETRY (UK, 1966)

THE MARCHES (1967)

COMMUNICATIONS (with Grandin Conover, 1970)

AVENUE OF THE AMERICAS (1971)

SANTIAGO POEMS (1975)

PROMETHEUS BOUND, Aeschylus (translation with C J
Herington, 1975, 1989)

QUECHUA PEOPLES POETRY (translation with Maria A
Proser, 1977, reissued 2007)

SCRAP BOOK (1977)

DE REPENTE / ALL OF A SUDDEN, Teresa de Jesus
(translation with Maria A Proser and Arlene Scully, 1979)

MAY DAY (1980)

APOLLO HELMET (1983)

LINE BREAK: POETRY AS SOCIAL PRACTICE (1988;
reissued 2005)

RAGING BEAUTY: SELECTED POEMS (1994)

WORDS WITHOUT MUSIC (2004)

James Scully, born 1937 in New Haven, CT, is a Professor
Emeritus of the University of Connecticut. He has received a
Lamont Award and a Guggenheim Fellowship. He was the
founding editor of Curbstone's "Art on the Line" series and
has published nine books of poetry, three works of translation
and two critical collections. His poetry appears in numerous
anthologies.

In 1973-1974, he and his family lived in Santiago de Chile,
during the first year of the Pinochet regime. This was
documented in *Santiago Poems* (1975), the first book
published by Curbstone, and an impetus for establishing the
Press.

He lives in San Francisco.

Curbstone Press, Inc.

is a non-profit publishing house dedicated to multicultural literature that reflects a commitment to social awareness and change, with an emphasis on contemporary writing from Latino, Latin American, and Vietnamese cultures.

Curbstone's mission focuses on publishing creative writers whose work promotes human rights and intercultural understanding, and on bringing these writers and the issues they illuminate into the community. Curbstone builds bridges between its writers and the public—from inner-city to rural areas, colleges to cultural centers, children to adults, with a particular interest in underfunded public schools. This involves enriching school curricula, reaching out to underserved audiences by donating books and conducting readings and educational programs, and promoting discussion in the media. It is only through these combined efforts that literature can truly make a difference.

Curbstone Press, like all non-profit presses, relies heavily on the support of individuals, foundations, and government agencies to bring you, the reader, works of literary merit and social significance that would likely not find a place in profit-driven publishing channels, and to bring these authors and their books into communities across the country.

If you wish to become a supporter of a specific book—one that is already published or one that is about to be published—your contribution will support not only the book's publication but also its continuation through reprints.

We invite you to support Curbstone's efforts to present the diverse voices and views that make our culture richer. Tax-deductible donations can be made to:
Curbstone Press, 321 Jackson Street, Willimantic, CT 06226
phone: (860) 423-5110   fax: (860) 423-9242
www.curbstone.org